New Jersey

The Brittingham Prize in Poetry

New Jersey

Betsy Andrews

The University of Wisconsin Press

The University of Wisconsin Press
1930 Monroe Street
Madison, Wisconsin 53711

www.wisc.edu/wisconsinpress/

3 Henrietta Street
London WC2E 8LU, England

1   3   5   4   2

Printed in the United States of America

Library of Congress Cataloging-in-Publication Data
Andrews, Betsy.
New Jersey / Betsy Andrews.
p.   cm. — (The Brittingham prize in poetry)
ISBN 0-299-22140-7 (alk. paper)
ISBN 0-299-22144-X (pbk.: alk. paper)
1. New Jersey — Poetry.   I. Title.
PS3601.N5526N49   2007
813'.6 — dc22   2006031436

You road I enter upon and look around,
I believe you are not all that is here,
I believe that much unseen is also here.

Walt Whitman, "Song of the Open Road"

Contents

Acknowledgments

The author thanks Furniture Press of Baltimore, Maryland, for publishing an excerpt of this work in pamphlet form. The author thanks the Julia and David White Colony of Cuidad Colon, Costa Rica, for the time and space to produce the bulk of this work. The author also thanks photographer Carolyn Monastra and musician Chandra Oppenheim for collaborating on a multimedia version of this work.

New Jersey

prowling down the ration line
in a state of poachers and hares
I wrote a note in pencil, and the turnpikeman,
a venturous fairy, promised to send it to you
it was the fetching of nuts, a staged comeback,
the highly discomfitting whisper of stars,
the exhalation of nativity figures,
a sordid drama new from the razor,
the smart highway's thousand sensors, altogether new
a new classification of birds and fishes
new potatoes, dug anew
the sluices, wharfs, wears, weirs, bucks, winches, dams, sasses,
floodgates wide open threw; it was gutter cleaning
a complaint, a jest, an intolerable grievance
loaded beyond the law
the new ice around us in thaw, the floating ice,
frazil ice, grease ice, pancake ice
it was of a specific gravity
winding like a snail cap up lee shores and frightful cliffs
words falling out like fillings
space like the space between thighs
an enormous moment, and a tiny thing
"It was fact-related," the official said.
a hove dance, a caroling,
it was cakes, child, cakes
composed entirely of zippers,
the sexed-up world's simple machine
a low bedeviling hum on a tarmac
that only some of us hear,

something no one writes about
unless they weren't there
miniscule, heartbreaking infant parts
sentences, sex, surveillance planes
a jackboot in the mouth
a family travel guide littered with filth
a snake who spits up a snoring dog
a bed creaking and creaking and creaking in the
crawl space behind the sheetrock
the text on a child's shopping bag:
if your heart is as kind as your young eyes now,
you are my love
hotrods and guitars, surfers and ravens, evergreens entrails and radio
girls in ranch house living rooms fraying like patchwork quilts

pure science's default gone "poof"
a crazy little lady picking reading material off windshields:
the history of semi-automatic sniper weapons, boy keeping place with his
    finger
a birthday card for a policing device, now entering its 'tweens
the laws of war that define when a structure ceases to be what it is claimed
    to be
and becomes a military target
a turkey dinner connoting trouble
a shaggy meteor prophesy, a slow boat slowly loading
a script of blackened girders in the whitewashed air

where symbols, of course, are extremely important
turns and nooks, mazes and hooks
the mouth wizardry of public pronouncements like,
We really hammered the place,
Major Darron Wright, 1st Battalion, 8th Infantry, 4th Infantry Division,
United States Army, Iraq.
Soldiers wearing night-vision goggles pouring in,
rifles at ready, streaming into bedrooms.
Women and children herded into one room, men into another.
The raid turns up nothing but a few World War II–era rifles, a sheaf of
     paper.
The lieutenant, a West Point graduate, pulls a wad of bills from his
     pocket,
peels off $120, hands it to one of the dazed men who signs a receipt for
     the reparations, and the soldiers troop back out.

while the cars in front of me move like gloved hands
humping along on haunches on little devil paws
I open my umbrella to the problem of the toll plaza,
electric lines, highway signs, overpass, guardrail, lamp standard, bridge
    structure, interchange, traffic advisory radio signals, microwave towers,
state police we know as police for their blue and white cars which read
    "police"

dual-dual roadway of inner and outer travel
stop, stretch, snack, rest with
the state's most famous citizens:
Walt Whitman: Oh Capt My Capt, Calamus, Cinnabon and an ATM
Richard Stockton: The Declaration of Independence, Blimpies and an
    ATM
Molly Pitcher: revolution, cross-dressing, Arthur Treacher's and an ATM
Grover Cleveland: the Sherman Act, the Pullman Strike, Carvel and an
    ATM
Thomas Alva Edison: the phonograph, the electric chair, Burger King and
    an ATM

misshapen skeleton fragments of noticing
cracked trees, refinery cranes, birds with suspiciously outsized ears
Who knows why we were on the lam?
It was the age of bombs and government secrets,
and I might have had something in my trunk
dog like a cat mewling, magnetically encoded toll ticket emitting its supple
    waves
notion of isolationism in tempered vision, molded petroleum, steel as
    buoyant as feather
but glass is a liquor, paint is an optics, axle a global account
spores blown in from Texas
nostalgia: a colonial disease
Washington's charges disembark barges, starve in their Hollow tents
a cigarette named Planet
a cigarette named American Spirit
a cigarette named More
plastic bags like animals moving
tourists fashioning key chains out of clouds with nothing in them
on the solipsistic shifting of lanes and the intimacy of bumper-to-bumper,
radio a backslide, a licensed unpacking of phrase
radio an exhaustion, a swan song of ruined gases and light,
feature: a software that forecasts genocide
feature: a woman who calls herself creature
feature: corpses in lime
Mars's moist hospitable past an alleged parallel universe
across the darkening sky's B-flat keening at 57 octaves below middle C
an 8-wheeled vehicle called Anger Management, an 8-wheeled vehicle
    called Ghost

from zero and in zero the true movement begins
a transplant of hands and mechanical fury
like the elephant whose lifelong keeper died
who took to the highway like breaking weather
the gulls in his blood diving diving at 500 beats per minute
who fell to his knees blown like a tire
he was yanked by a chain back to the barracks
ambushed by a booster of vitamin E the size of national defense

amid the boom in triple-wide caskets and ready-built houses you can hold
     in your hand
well-fed Americans pilfer the turn-off mini-markets
twirling bottles of sauce overhead, running for the door
in the sudden rearview mirror, I have grey hair, blue eyes, a small historical
     moustache
I am calling myself Fritz
wheels southbound and rolling from straddling the orphan girl's thick cock
questions decamping the vinyl roof
like helicopter, like Canada geese, the wind becoming an "it"
candidates sipping their pancake house fortunes, six lolloping lips
eyeball damage, earlobe damage
chain bookstore employees wrapped in bandages blazing like flesh
"What is needed is a little smacky face," says the unnamed intelligence
     officer.
aquamarine lace panty and bra set the assassinated lover would've gone for

from northern meadowlands to southern farmlands

soybeans, peaches, eggplants, onions, peppers, beans, asparagus, apples, cranberries, blueberries, strawberries, corn, New Jersey's 800 million tomatoes,

poison insects tiny bombs fields of chemical shit

Navy Combat System Engineering rising from the toxic dung

small scrap of lover on the dirty car floor

old dog in the back seat minding her old tricks

reports that nothing has happened yet, not

screaming old ladies, motorized carts, luggage left on carousels, babies crawling on glass

crisps of curl off wild winch whirl

at the lady poets' potluck, the endearing father figure

tapes a poem to my face,

like a captive forced to march the streets holding my bars up in front of me,

I troop to the groaning board where the drunken friend takes a bite of the thing,

spits it out transformed

behind the sonic barricades
cordoning off the casualty roll call from
Pennsville, Westville, Groveville, Yardville,
Robbinsville, Belleville, Bernardsville, Somerville
a moment of happiness in a heap in the road
a calendar year where 10 days go missing
"This stuff doesn't happen in New Jersey,"
says the wrangler of pesky coincidence,
the trooper shedding his skin;
not 400 homes 600 yards from the peacekeepers' camp aflame
not crocodiles mobbing the Senate floor
not furred, scaled, clawed, fanged, sealed and otherwise off-putting
    documents
man holds the world in his palm, placed there by mechanised transport
a flock of planetessimals pop like gooseberries under the diamond
    merchant's thumb,
a certain artlessness slick with gravity
half a million birds along an 80-mile stretch

in a universe that looks like a multicar wreck
a silo of sewage exploding
fatal ticks on the devil's face
that 30-second dislocation when
the place you've lived in half your life is suddenly rendered unknown,
a run-in with a speed trap disguised as a pair of enormous breasts,
like the elephants who hijack sugarcane trucks
one elephant plays dumb in the road
the rest of the elephants gorge themselves
Woodrow Wilson: Prohibition, The League of Nations, Pizza Hut and an
    ATM
the head of international espionage the last speaker of a dying language,
"We are chasing people all the time, and we're doing it better and better."
As in "actively engaged in setting the conditions for
successful exploitation of the detainees," General D. Miller,
classified recommendation, American detention camp, Guantánamo Bay
blueprints for towers with trusses that shred oncoming planes like paper
monks on an island *enquiring tenderly, . . . anxious to know if we were*
    engaged in any war

at the Swedesboro exit, at the Woodbury exit, at the Camden exit, at the
     Burlington exit
hometown thespians rehearse a musical adaptation of war games,
the deadeye indicator of the devil, undazzled, in the details
a bus full of party delegates slouching in their friction-charged skins
rolls past the jobbing line, rolls past the meat-packing plant
toward the birth of a new convulsive nature, a countrywide husbandry,
an emotional swing, the dream of the dream of the dream of a driver,
seated and commandeering down the gaping streets of retractable housing
where the aluminum siding licks its own wounds,
and a four-year-old in the driveway
repeats to herself, *you're okay, you're okay*

the rewiring of the moods of birds expensive and three-dimensional
a parting gift from the Pentagon
a car exhaust full in the face
an aggressive opinion from the arbiter of lawn-based accidents
a truck blasted to skin and bones at a wildly inaccurate longitude
12,351 objections to the most enigmatic of scandals:
why one gruesome business transaction is favored against another
an everyday phenomenon that brings on an insulting degree of fervor
"Sweet child. He doesn't have a clue,"
says the grandmother heaving the perambulator
past the tunnel mouth filling with smoke
a phalanx of speedboats racing upriver to guard the interstate bridges
a shit-flinging gravitas that makes generals quiver
the flavor of McDonald's in a place called The Love Room
in a wing that the incarcerated "aspire to get to," Colonel Nelson J.
    Cannon,
commander of joint detention operations, Camp X-Ray, Guantánamo
    Bay,
"We try to keep people hopeful."

in Hightstown, in Hornerstown, in Hackettstown, in Bordentown
catharsis in a screaming evangelathon
on a narrow strip of Weehawken cliff, a conspiracy of pins and needles
    and burrs
Alexander Hamilton: The Federalist, the Treasury, Roy Rogers and an
    ATM
in the temporary toilet, conception
in plastic name tag, disposable gloves and paper hat
while the massive governor's exempted toys belch up inert regulations
It wasn't the weigh-station blow job that got him,
it was the bubble-child deflating.
dog squats on my depth of field, beady-eyed, drooling and panting
the homeowner prays for the truck driver
speeding by, fixing his fly ten yards from the bedroom window
"I'm an ant," the homeowner says, "the Turnpike is an elephant."

Turnpike immaculate, the salt marsh flanked in
masks, cupids, urns, plumage, syringes, food wrappers, cigarette butts,
the carved and gilded heraldry of a clean-up crew called Special Removal,
leasing themselves like automobiles registered to a series of dummy
    corporations
wraparound ballistics the belief in an extraordinary rendition of
the axiom *let every soul be subject*

privatization privatized, the government document humped
beyond bearing with noisily disappearing ink,
"One well-stocked 7-Eleven could knock out 30 Iraqi stores,"
enthuses the amply endowed consultant,
"a Wal-Mart could take over the country."
the dog's tail cropped in one howling chop pet-named Order 39
I'm a card person, I'm a card person,
I sang in the beautiful dream of surveillance
tits hanging out at the underground party,
allegiance to god and country the password
at the trapdoor to the long shaft down
a vast fantasy factory:
emotional shifts bar-coded
and scanned like packaged lettuce
a passenger train made of mosquitoes
a tremor the size of a victory lap
an after-hours orgy at the faith-healing bank,
whipped cream smeared on the manager's lips
"It's importance to the defense effort is obvious,"
speechifies the governor, hands up the Turnpike's twat
as the elephant opens his one good eye,
to see that the rest of the zoo has been eaten

a new prison atop the old prison
a spectre that haunts the marshlands seared in molten blacktop
So departed the new knights on their way to
the next unfortunate village,
the new-dug graves an environment
not half so strange as the new-peopled streets.
across the rash-fresh seas where the new trout run,
a Jersey worsened by the tusk-risen beast
of the evening report beaten into submission
the knitting of a staple industry
amalgamated silence, universally worn

slow lane a mythos,
a leash attached to a wire run
ending just short of a strip search
the Turnpike a constant snapping apart
a constant pounding together
new relationships between scattered forms
like circus clowns thrown from an unmarked car
Lake Surprise, Lake Success, Thundergust, Oxford Furnace, Swartswood,
     Rising Sun, Little Tank Pond, Big Tank Pond cobwebbing in the
     quasi-governmental winter light
surfaces cracking and booming, above the same cold fish with the same
     banging bite
night-shriek Turnpike, legs like a crane, wings like a bat, face like a horse,
     tail like a fork
hoofprints on the snowy roofs, tearing farmers' chickens to pieces
dogs too scared to follow its tracks
mills and factories stoppered and shut
telephone linemen chased up their poles
trolleymen in New Brunswick and Trenton arming themselves to the
     teeth
mob with pistols and pitchforks and rakes cutting a line through the forest
professional people beyond reproach in Mount Misery, in Double Trouble
taking the Turnpike, deformed and immortal,
for an uncanny herald of great global conflict
while the handful of passengers on the Paterson & Hudson River line
scurry out to drag the locomotive from the muck,
one of them pausing to shoot at a turtle
beneath the holographic coming of highway

talk of arming the tollbooths
troopers in badges cribbed from West Point
a five-minute deluge of mud and dead fish, the Drunk-O-Meter dial
     tripped
at the monthly Rebuild Iraq trade show
in the Sportsplex splayed on 11,000 acres of cindered pines
holes in the floor like nostrils flaring with technicians ducking misgivings
like an elephant pricked with a sharp stick so she jumps on her chains
     looking fearsome
pachyderm feed the promise of an unobstructed viewpoint,
of substantial horizontal and vertical clearances,
of the utter extinction of curves,
of bridges so understated that motorists never dream of a river
of the obsolescence of strict limitations on a statesmanlike delectation
to have anyone indefinitely detained

in Chesterfield, in Mansfield, in Haddonfield, in Plainfield
a new face on the old face squinting and talking anew of
snarling roadblocks, body cavities, identity checks, palm grease
a microscopic incision in the car's metal skin,
militancy pouring in
the pathology tale of the simply broke goes marching off to war
Drake equations (hurrah, hurrah), Doppler effects,
photinos and squarks and selectrons be gone
in light of what a pilot whale has in common with the national missile
    defense system:
neither of them can distinguish a Mylar balloon from appropriate targets,
an argument on the futility of meaning taken apart by
an elderly lady who doubles as an underfed dog
at the meeting of people who can't pay their bills, a blemish sprouts on a
    cheek
while from here the buildings look like candy,
from here they look like passport stamps
and the blondes and brunettes look like terra-cotta soldiers
and the grass around the comfort station looks like a place to jerk off,
the Giant Voice coaxing with deals on rocket launch tubes, on AK-47s
the all-you-can-eat Dionysian buffet of the world's every known greeting
seized by a bureaucrat with a phraselator barking "Put your hands on the
    wall"

curtain up on the new set in stone in Camden, Edison, Rahway, Linden
a glossy coffee-table tome on the history of dug-in bunkers
military checkpoints in corridor cities the staple cocktail background
for an epoch of security clearance
the ambassador of draconian counsel a guy who's "kind of fun to be
    around"
graciousness a moth-eaten ball,
"gentle" a modifier detained
a blank check for blueprints in the vernacular of a worldwide trap
prison records in pigeon shit,
the killing cure in a gas mask
worst-case scenarios outsourced like Ivan the Terrible's architects' eyes
the help-desk representative wriggles in her warm bucket seat
burping up White Out onto her outfit, the functional equivalent of a
    bulletproof vest
on her desk an improvised explosive device as scrumptious as a bowl of
    cookies
the Turnpike, skirt of serpents, swallows the twitching day,
a prey as fat as the alert orange jaws are able to unkilter
New Jersey is a ho-ho bird,
a fantastical creature ingested with shock-inducing ostentation,
like the operatic death of an elephant, shedding its jumpsuit, gasping for
    air,
the traffic is a comet, a colicky baby wailing disaster
at best speed toward the open casket,
the saved face pumped full of anti-rejection drugs,
flush with civilian defense dollars,
stuffed with bullhorns, headlamps and booster rockets,
back-up emergency radio, decontamination tents

while on the rubbled shore by the gutter runoff,
a tern lifts crumbs of Styrofoam
gingerly to her chicks' open beaks,
thinking the stuff fish eggs

pintail season, mallard season, canvasback season, goldeneye season
New Jersey meadow reversal of fortune,
a school with punt guns for windows
a woman who's paid to have her feet disassembled
a plague of styrene cups
a sandwich that tastes like torn tickets
a sandwich that tastes like hands on knees
wigeon season, gadwall season, bufflehead season, ruddy duck season
the season of the PCB skeleton dress, the season of the quarantined public
substantial funds for a study of migratory predators' aversion to cages
steel shot, bismuth shot, tungsten-iron-nickel-tin shot
"I was infantry. We blew things up. I felt that my heart was in the right
    place,"
Tristan Wyatt, amputee, hit with a rocket-propelled hand grenade, August
    25, 2003,
3rd Armored Calvary Regiment, United States Army, Iraq
woodcock season, shoveler season, clapper rail season, common snipe
    season
in the darkened museum, the darkened hides of the elephants stuffed,
    lifelike

"to the victor, the spoils," quoth the Beltway insider,
"and in this case, the spoils are choosing who governs"
lying inside the circular argument of its federally funded roadbed,
the southern city of monuments assumes a magical transfer of power
knifing into the quickening sands for caisson disease, for ancient sea carcass
on the desk of the one-armed immigration bandit, paperwork building up,
while muscling down the cracked back of this blasted old cunt of a garden,
a bag of garbage burning in the breakdown lane of her potty mouth,
I am whoring poetry from fashion, from smashing-sad bills of sale
from the burning desire for a bone-cold tenth planet
from the exploding cigar of the dead artist's continuing success
I am whoring off election buns and frying pans and castle moats
off the eruptions on the abdomens of the boxcars in the Conrail yard:
ACLX, NATX, UTLX, XXXX, off distancing articles as well, as the
    Americans
poach contraband Polaroids off the salt-beard jaw of Elizabeth, thinking
    the
largest containerized freight facility on the bought and sold and bought
    and sold globe
handsome in the liminal sun, where buried streams run acetone and
    trichloroethylene
the in-between, the ramble on, the move along, the here-and-gone
vomiting a goddamn through a city where the neighbor's kid sinks in a
    drainage ditch
patrols disguised as carpet bags, stitched
with the wrinkles in the highway's racial profile,
pale Authority's vested nest, yolk its eminent domain

the provisional authority of a swamp flower
that mimics insects in order to eat insects
ragged fringe, dragon's mouth, knodding lady's tresses,
grass pink, prince of the Pinelands, wild lupine, shoe of Venus pucker
     vicarious lips
at the sundew staging a bang-bang stick-'em-up takedown of a gnat,
a series of concentric cataracts as tacky as an executive order
the dwarf pines taking to poverty like a backhoe takes to the dirt
unearthing the new probability, unearthing the new decay
new lords, new laws, New Thingers doing their new thing: thinging
breaking out in a wildly inexplicable interest in seasonality
the first symptom of a directional ho; eastward this time,
toward the new flagellation, gravitational forces collapsing
into the same old forms
with heavy-metal philosophy, with new heavy-metal burn
driving, rallying, chasing, stalking, flushing the turning worm
a town that homebakes vehicle armor
a town afloat like a sink box

unity another name for plunging into the Raritan
the Passaic River, Toms River, the Hackensack River, the Hudson River
Potter's Creek, Berry's Creek, Oyster Creek, Hope Creek
hopelessly bound to the captains of industry,
flipping their toxic pocket change, a migrating plume of a self-fulfilled
   wish
minted of arsenic, mercury, cyanide, zinc, plutonium, chromium, cesium,
   tritium,
benzene, toluene, naphthalene, phenanthrene, methylene chloride, lead
"Some mistakes were made in the past,"
wags the tongue of historic pollutions
haunting the heirloomed baby teeth, haunting the Kill van Kull
the Muddabuck Creek, Doctor Creek, Shit Creek, Dead Creek
an electrode up the ass of a black widow spider
a graveyard of plastic bouquets
a military hovel called elephant
a website called "Where to Shoot"
a full-depth, roving wiretap
from Deepwater's southern holster to Ridgefield's northern spur
headless pirates, Tories and Hessians, smugglers, bootleggers, Hansel und
   Gretel
in a bog coined Patriot Act, Section 215: surveillance agents in hot-mix
   heat
gnawing the Jersey Barriers, feeding on "any tangible thing"

warehouses heated by the burning of scrolls in Tenafly, in Cedar Grove
the loss of mammoth libraries the attorney general's ashen craft
as a lobbyist called Il Duce rolls up the wilderness, trucks it bye-bye
down the closed-door negotiable fast lane under a chemical compound
    called sky
where campaign contributions plug a pothole so large that it alters
    perspective
as on the morning radio talk show, torture doubles for fun
as the vastly supersize office park opens, leaks its chilled air in the sun

"Should I shoot him, sir? Should I blast his head?" said the soldier to his
    commander,
the commander's reply a geometry with no real shape at all
a frontier abstraction with the biomass of a herd of cardboard bison
a western filmed in New Jersey
the lack of fiction in stone soup
locust storms and chaos theory and pedal to the metal
the American idiom's getaway car
the hotwire ignition bypass that underlies the nightly sign-off
a UN truck filled with bad mathematics
a bean that eats at the nerves
pits spit from an elephant's trunk
a bakery serving mud
a half-gassed dog twitching its leg on the Meadowlands' last open landfill
a windsock, an air horn, a methane vent, a pneumatic drill
a heroic apocrypha labeled Plan B
the suburban forbearance of sidewalks
a meteor shower in a potter's field
decommissioned weaponry sprinkled on the grass
a rampart of bile and humors and fits
an uncontrollable muscle contraction,
the sound of one hand wringing
a detour around the spot-check
a help-wanted ad for a cause célèbre of extreme intent
"just a little vial of something," offers the National Security Advisor
the actuarial reckoning of a substantial sum for an equities trader
(rather more substantial than the sum for a fire chief)
a prisoner nicknamed Half-Dead Bob, a prisoner nicknamed Al Qaeda
    Claus

blackout goggles, a hood and shackles, and after, a nice game of chess
an air conditioner as a penal contrivance
reverse gear on a fumigated field
a terrified cock-a-doodle-doo
a village where nobody tends to the stalls, where nobody moves in the
    alleys
an equation that's only half-complete until the air turns rancid

from the fire tower at Apple Pie Hill, a smoke screen thrown up off the
    dubious desert
weapons of mass destruction the bogeyman's piss in the sink
"And Abraham Lincoln was short," says the United States Secretary of
    Defense
Albert Freeman Africanus King, attendant to the fatal coupling,
Lincoln and Lincoln's bullet,
weaving the southern city of monuments a monumental hairpiece
to keep the blood-sucking solicitors at bay
from the fire tower at Bearfort Ridge, comes the malarial airborne
then dragonfly a transparent ploy, then incision of a slippery 'rat,
then the well-masked, well-enumerated, coffer-raiding raccoon,
then the full-frontal nudity of a town car,
a naked smack in the face of the bandit who crosses the highway too soon
the green-zone chip on the turnpike's shoulder,
a fine kettle for the turkey vulture, digesting a corpse-worth of anthrax,
a word related to coal, dirty meal of the dirty old rail that pales next to
    strontium-90
workers pissing a motherfuck into the power plant core
plumes off the heads of New Jersey egrets, plumes in the caps of
    Washington whores

a mathematician in a fabulous wig
nags an oyster for obvious answers
turtles beheaded by oncoming manias,
the lack of the hypothetical,
the entire world bound at the wrists
the go-go joint muse of the morning truth
in a thong full of slugs for the toll bridge
the palming of a stone in a synthetic fist
thousands of prosthetic options:
a chair and rings for shackles,
a hand afterwards for cracking a beer
a shrewd group calculus
plagiarized from a fodder for sheep
disguised as declarative statements of self
politician shooting blanks at the camera,
the factual melting in "cheese"
carburetion, lubrication, the moveable feast cobbled together
from fat bits of leftover bulk mail and piquant communiqués
a feedbag for power that hits the ground running
a homespun medusa-like dinner bell
a benediction known as the choke
the populace torque-converting on a trick rubber loin chop
labeled "It's best to leave well enough alone."

communitas an iris scan
a sales pitch with opulent shock
a commercial spin-off of a grave breach of conduct
with a constant demand for spare parts
across the sweeping silent treatment of the organophosphate lawn
a citizenry bathed in starlight, the halogen stars turned on
artificial gravity a beautiful, thick-skinned device
against the cluster bombs of the souvenir photos of the cellblock in the
    desert night
America is a friend of all the Iraqi people, Abu Ghraib prison, Iraq
body invasion, sleep deprivation, humiliation, isolation, temperature
    alteration,
noise infiltration, asphyxiation, canine persuasion, intimidation
"I can't give you any more information,"
says the Secretary of Defense of the United States,
"because I don't—I've forgotten."

real-time images beamed back to base
ransacked street grid a gut check upon
the mangy dogma that wags the tale that
watching the batter and being the batter are one and the same thing
at second base, the hospitality crew unfolds a half-baked cakewalk
at first base, somebody spells the word "blitz"
a piston machine made out of humans
enormous white geese lifting off in V-formation from the unseemly crash
broken dashes, hoary edges, mourning cloaks, metalmarks, tawny
    emperors,
fiery skippers, harvesters, dogfaces, great spangled frippery,
confused cloudywings take to the air amid
spheres of oil, cylinders of oil, pyramids of oil, cubes of oil
glittering scum on production's great ocean
tanker a blubbering ghoul
spill lit by a fifth-order decoy affixed to a puncture-proof pardon
the near-blind eye in the done-wronged landscape
the near-blind eye of forgotten Hog Wallow, Speedwell, Prospertown,
    Waretown, Brindle Town, Sweetwater, Slabtown, at sparkplug
    intervals falling upon
crankshaft, crankpin, piston ring, flywheel, driving plate, driven plate,
    sliding gear, clutch
on panoptic cameras, on billboard seductions, on radar, on well-concealed
    rules,
a vastness cluttered with private rockets, a vastness that ends in a blast wall
the marbled base of an elephant's foot, an election of bricks, a fog bank
headlights out now; the highway's gunned wink,
hair of the dog a trigger

virtually unwelcome at the national family motel
where the asphalt vamps cheap and loose for pay-by-the-hour parking
my head is a color transfer hacked into the pillow
mattress ticking a fax of my inflammatory form
in the bedside nightstand middle drawer, a sinewy, chain-smoking text
in the top drawer, claustrophobia:
a manual for the appearance of service, uniform ass to snout
white people on the television playing white people
on a mountain, playing white people at the beach
commercial for a doctor-prescribed rat-a-tat-tat of nuh-uh,
jingle injecting addiction, an accelerator labeled "legacy"
AM alarm clock shock wave a doughnut baked at Mach 1
from the abandoned future highwayside hamlet
an odor as if from another world we were never intended to notice
nothing but closets and toilets left standing, a gale-force exurbanity
"the furniture should not be startling" read the subsidized
interrogation guidelines, "pictures should be missing or dull"
the dog scales the upholstery, the autobiography of a shut-in
who senses in eleven dimensions

New Jersey topography hypodermic
state bird a lingering sting
across the junk-rolled nautical miles
the occulting light, the first-order flashing, the front range beacon,
the spherical lamps, the bivalve lens, the signal boys black out
overdosing on obfuscation Shooter's Island, Corner Stake, Elbow of Cross,
Wreck Pond, the hypocritical Point Comfort, the hypocrite Navesink
the dark seahorse of a wartime dilution of the actual shoals, the actual reefs
the body politic a watermark
except for the wraiths of the radium factory who lesion the shipping veins
leading Marines to the Five Fathom trough with their working girl
    phosphorescence

the luminous hands on the sentinel's watch turning turning turning and
turning like elephants around an abandoned mill,
blinkered and uncomprehending
old Bill Miller ridin' on the tiller steering round the Browertown Bend;
old Davy Ross with a ten dollar hoss comin' up the Pompton Plane
canal boats stopped at the rusted locks on Morristown's terminal moraine
rusted canned water in the fallout shelter next to the "kiddie kokoon"
rusted Kalashnikov on the market blanket, rusted Humvee in the lagoon
elephants enduring the blizzard-raw Alps, blinkered and uncomprehending

facial recognition software a guarded form of intimacy
nature replaced by naturized recreation zones,
new lands founded by the messengers of the kings,
prewashed, destemmed and treated for color retention
traffic at a standstill like an elephant on a treadmill
the road by this means continually warmed as to make for a scalding
    matter
candied confessions, caustic prayers, meted suspicions, babble
tall white hats revisited
the concern voiced abroad an ancient and smelly goat
New Jersey houses daily-dipped in the mudge-green glow of tactical
    broadcast,
a fraction of procedural doctrine that seasons into whole forests cleared
five billion dollars this month, five billion dollars the next
as the wobbly inmates return to their cells
"It fried them," says the official.

Turnpike a bottleneck
bursting like locusts, like tiny stars,
an unanswerable echo
a cherry bomb dropped on a denuded hill
where the cut-rate mall drains the till
of the local want-some want-some
a glove box filled with mystery contracts
a dashboard swarming with wish lists
a pacemaker, a defibrillator, an armored unit called "light"
a wildcat strung from an oil derrick
dripping and dripping and dripping
a state shaped like an hourglass,
a state shaped like a woman,
trucks for tamping tamping and tamping
flatbeds, lowboys, minesweepers
a healthy bout of humping at the Vince Lombardi meat rack
a "god's-eye-view" of the battle
the new global trade in very bad guys
an elephant on antidepressants,
an elephant with herpes
a whip one hundred miles long
the panic behavior in chickens
infantry in exoskeletons, painless as crustaceans
"It's fun to shoot some people," muses the three-star general
as the thorn-tongued Turnpike falls on fresh fields
in the near-hottest year on record

"We're an empire now," says the senior advisor. "We create our own
    reality,"
like agribusiness, like blood in the mouth
like a meal that resembles a reconnaissance map
like apple pie–scented room spray, like breakfast cereal as hopped-up as
    crack
like a travesty dumbed down to a heartwarming coda
like red and white and blue bric-a-brac
like gun-toting men in the camel market
like scorched-earth campaigns, like internal displacement
like sandstorm on the devil's clock brewing brewing brewing and brewing
like soldiers deployed from Fort Dix, from Fort Monmouth,
from Earle Naval Weapons Station, from McGuire Air Force Base
the vice president breathless over the "nasty" beauty of the "dark side"

by the damp hairs of the comatose,
by the hairs-on-end of the dead,
500 pink sweet williams sprout in the justice's flower-beds,
lice corralling, scratching and sniffing
like there's black gold in the body's warm folds,
like it's one big-ass Texas
a view of a single human as rich as the furthest satellite's access
a notion of first obscurity, like a minister dating a sin
but still no definitive date as to when the naked maneuvers began
the wind blows a revelry through the dry-cleaning store
almost rousing the unclaimed uniform, knocking it to the floor
an enigma beamed from somewhere between the mountaintop and the
    murk
programs the labyrinth of booby-trapped speed bumps between home
    and work
in a place where cops duck behind ski masks or lie on a ward and moan
they count to 1000 in prime numbers only: inedible chickens
from the egg, nothing but bone
while here Fingerprint and Criminal Records,
Auto Theft Bureau,
License Bureau,
Photographic Unit,
Corruption Unit,
Missing Persons,
Laboratory of Forensic Science,
Criminal Enterprise and Racketeering,
Organized Crime Task Force Bureau,
Marine Law Enforcement Bureau,
State Police Metro Crime Task Force,

Gambling Enforcement and Casino Control,
Hazardous Waste Background Investigation Unit,
Narcotics, Polygraph and Intelligence Squads
rove only New Jersey alone

mining the savage electional hour
the motorcade of monstrous mandate
ferries the hard-coin incumbent
from the site of the Battle of Paulus Hook
to the site of the Battle of Red Bank
logging the miles in a galling suit
promising middling fortunes
it's a new entire, the castle rising,
fugue state come on at a hair-raising speed,
10,000 bad smells at once
photoluminescent paint striping
the electrified fence between points
on a map of screws, rotten eggs and hedges
the magic eye registering
a pack of starving nonce-words
chasing the dummy hare of salvation
to his next easy win
"In a large society
the election of a monarch
can never devolve to the wisest,"
Edward Gibbon, *The Decline and
Fall of the Roman Empire,* 1776
insurgency as a form of employ
a red and white and blue tradition
minutemen in their underwear
storming Congressional Hall for back pay
while at the bottom of the second column to the right
New Jersey's founding fathers—
the homosexual harpsichordist

the reverend plucking his eyebrows—
are sealed in glass and bronze and gas
like taxidermied roadkill
as in the course of human events
the motorcade pauses to fill its tanks
with a wish list for corporate investors

the thirteenth infernal child, I am looping down the on-ramps
exile of eleven newly purchased hostile States:
the State of stinking two-by-twos and noiseless taunts
the State of softball gospel and fuzzy denouements
the State of blues sewn like blankets trimmed in tar-and-feather thrills
the saturated State of vicious pelts and interior combustible ills
the State of confederate geometry and melancholy flight
the State of bitter-rooted skies and elevated blight
the State of exhumed hatchets and oxymoronic larks
the State of eerie visitation and rubberneck remarks
the desicated State of scissored holidays and seminal bluffs
the State of gaping questions and exploitable, hard-knock trust
the State of mournful chorus calls and uproarious latter-day briefs
the little rabbit snuggles in her little reinforced concrete cage,
no qualms about having mortgaged so close to the strafing range

as a brand-name jet luckies-up into the ponderous Newark airspace
a platinum blonde muskrat scratches her belly along the slick sand
the dumb mechanics of unawares to fines, floggings, solitary confinement
the implicated hardware, the unaccountably soft pest share a geography
    sharpened by a dead battery, like a tooth grown inside of a nest
coot season, blue goose season, ring-necked season, brant season
one feathered wing still attached, the kill is taken
to the migratory bird preservation station, kind words for a bucket of guts
Clara Barton: the Franco-Prussian War, the American Red Cross, TCBY
    and an ATM
the Turnpike made place replacing places,
bridge a screwpile tossed across has-beens
antennae conjunctified eyes
fuck-me shoes on the gas station sink board
death by chemical toilet
a convertible top made of stolen IDs
a nudie on the bumper of the dump truck hauling mildewed psalms
a boat in the reeds almost Egyptian
"We are like birds in a cage," says Yasin Mustafa, school teacher, Abu
    Hishma, Iraq
"This fence is here for your protection. Do not approach or try to cross,
    or you will be shot," says the sign on the barbed-wire fence, Abu
    Hishma, Iraq
the flatbed tipping up like a sexpot
road crew in orange hard hats taking instruction from a little machine

flyover ramp, bypass, hazard warning, speed limit sign, closed-circuit TV
are no guarantee against the metallic taste of the sauce break
in a mixing bowl of divergent intent
"We don't give our cops nightsticks
for ornaments," says Jersey City's boss
the swamp drops its trashy eyelid
sucks the highway supports like a cock

(half of the deer live on the mountain
half the deer live on the plain
when they meet in the foothills, it is only to talk
they are deer after all, not humans)   .

the law against walking hits and runs
like the grope-grope departure gate bon voyage
like arrival's finger-yank hi there to
a nation of corn belts and wheat belts and rust belts
where a widow adopts a box of frozen food
so she can eat when she's hungry
a habit broken, a habit renewed: the boom in electrical prodding
the moving idea a cloverleaf plucked in the rush-hour gridlock to war
the nation's first commander-in-chief swallowing fish from a long-gone
    stock,
blood-leech crazy and cursing until the leaves on the trees rock
Miss Inter-City Beauty Maid, sash like a vaulted Skyway, turns heel
on an old and cruel method for keeping pigs pastured
on the petrified skin of the lacquer works and the melon yards and the
    mothball plant
car riveted to the moon-tide rise,
valving and gearing slipping on the spleen between charged bodies
in the molten depths of the smoldering dump, anxiety a cooling solid
the fallen done in by more than the breeze, the neck host to more than
    one rope burn
stones in a gland with nerves of great size and a pirated handle: Point-
    No-Point

it's a glimpse of space through an 8-foot straw
the assisted revival of a deadly disease
extended combat deployment for dolphins
a bird that nests in a chain-sawed tree,
dancing for a mate in the dust

on a sky built of squares in a city emptied of contents
someone's dinner on the freezing concrete,
gravy like hunks of glass
the dog kidnaps thoughts off my plate,
ugly food poorly plated,
taking the middle of America by storm
James Fenimore Cooper: The Last of the Mohicans, Popeyes and an ATM
Joyce Kilmer: Trees and Other Poems, Nathans and an ATM
context in which a "lavatory"
context in which "nighttime fixins' bar technician" the unretiree
car parking, truck parking, bus parking poured upon
oak, birch, beech, maple, hemlock, dogwood, white cedar, pine
upon white-tailed deer, upon fox, upon squirrel, upon chipmunk, upon
    bear
(a few fewer bear),
upon woodchuck, possum, rattlesnake, skunk, upon Jersey blue, that fat
    mongrel fowl,
various performance-enhancing additives locked into a mass poured
over limestone, sandstone, gneiss, schist, shale, granite, marble, slate,
    basalt
above it all: heaven, a military gain
beneath it all: a map on the wall
a label that reads "Our World"
a presidential Plutonian suite upholstered in
brawling, warrior swagger swatches of aggressively hot pink

like the poem I found in the State of the Union:
terror
       terrorist
terrorists
       terrorists
terrorists
       terrorists
terrorist
       terror
terrorism
       terrorists
terrorists
       terrified
terror
       terrorist
the takeover boys, the property boys, I mean, these people are serious

and I am hoggishly, wolfishly, piggishly, doggedly
harebrained, Hegelian, schoolish of course,
but love storms my middle-aged lips,
in the new moon, the new-old solution
the bleachers like bellows breathing with the breath of the breathing
  people
light thrown off in all directions
it's enough to give one goose-flesh,
or else wrap tissue around the tabloids
that way, the news won't rub off on you

Feeder Lanes

The Oxford English Dictionary; The New York Times; Mother Jones Magazine; Harper's Magazine; National Public Radio; The Associated Press; Reuters; the BBC; *The New Yorker; The Atlantic Monthly; New York Magazine;* Encarta '96; United States Department of Defense news transcripts; Donald Rumsfeld; Dick Cheney; Condoleezza Rice; George W. Bush; Gerard Manley Hopkins; David Bowie; George Gordon, Lord Byron; Elsa Schiaparelli; Sarah Jessica Parker; various U.S. soldiers serving in Iraq, various Iraqi civilians; the eleven of the United States that passed anti-gay marriage referendums in the 2005 elections: Arkansas, Georgia, Kentucky, Michigan, Mississippi, Montana, North Dakota, Ohio, Oklahoma, Oregon, Utah; numerous anonymous government officials and secret memos, C.I.A. and F.B.I. operatives; numerous detainees; my dreams; my dog; my car; my route home to Philadelphia; the official website of the New Jersey Turnpike; the official website of the State of New Jersey; the official website of the New Jersey State Police; the official website of the New Jersey Department of Environmental Protection, Division of Fish & Wildlife, especially as it pertains to the subject of hunting; New Jersey, the map, prepared by the State of New Jersey Department of Transportation in cooperation with the U.S. Department of Transportation Federal Highway Administration and distributed free by the State of New Jersey through the United States Postal System; websites on the subject of the Jersey Devil, including theshadowlands.net and elktownship.com/myth; the wildflower fact sheet at hoganphoto.com; website of the Northern

Prairie Wildlife Research Center, Butterflies of New Jersey page; website of the New Jersey Lighthouse Society; websites of the Asphalt Institute and the National Asphalt Pavement Association; *The Secret House: The Extraordinary Science of the Ordinary Day*, by David Bodanis; *Looking for America on the New Jersey Turnpike*, by Angus Kress Gillespie and Michael Aaron Rockland; *The New Jersey Colony*, by Dennis Brindell Fradin; *New Jersey History*, by Peter Kross; *New Jersey Firsts*, by Harry Armstrong and Tom Wilk; *The Meadowlands: Wilderness Adventures on the Edge of the City*, by Robert Sullivan; *Forgotten Mills of Early New Jersey*, by Harry and Grace M. Weiss; *Old Canals of New Jersey*, by Richard F. Veit; *Quiet Water of New Jersey*, by Kathy Kenley; *Nature Walks in New Jersey*, by Glenn Scherer; *Body Toxic: An Environmental Memoir*, by Susanne Antonetta; "The U.S. Patriot Act: What Writers Need to Know," by Kay Murray, general counsel and assistant director of the Author's Guild, *Poets & Writers Magazine*, October/November 2004.

The Brittingham Prize in Poetry
Ronald Wallace, General Editor

Places/Everyone • Jim Daniels
C. K. Williams, Judge, 1985

Talking to Strangers • Patricia Dobler
Maxine Kumin, Judge, 1986

Saving the Young Men of Vienna • David Kirby
Mona Van Duyn, Judge, 1987

Pocket Sundial • Lisa Zeidner
Charles Wright, Judge, 1988

Slow Joy • Stephanie Marlis
Gerald Stern, Judge, 1989

Level Green • Judith Vollmer
Mary Oliver, Judge, 1990

Salt • Renée Ashley
Donald Finkel, Judge, 1991

Sweet Ruin • Tony Hoagland
Donald Justice, Judge 1992